SOUTH DEVON

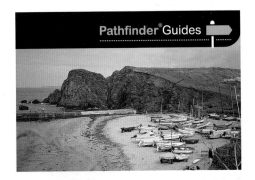

Pathfinder®Guides

Short Walks

Compiled by Brian Conduit
Revised by Sue Viccars

Acknowledgements

My thanks to Devon County Council and the various tourist information centres throughout the area.

Text:	Brian Conduit Revised text for 2009 and 2017 editions, Sue Viccars
Photography:	Brian Conduit, Sue Viccars. Front cover: © Howard Taylor/Alamy Stock Photo
Editorial:	Ark Creative (UK) Ltd
Design:	Ark Creative (UK) Ltd

ISBN: 978-0-31909-092-3

While every care has been taken to ensure the accuracy of the route directions, the publishers cannot accept responsibility for errors or omissions, or for changes in details given. The countryside is not static: hedges and fences can be removed, stiles can be replaced by gates, field boundaries can alter, footpaths can be rerouted and changes in ownership can result in the closure or diversion of some concessionary paths. Also, paths that are easy and pleasant for walking in fine conditions may become slippery, muddy and difficult in wet weather, while stepping stones across rivers and streams may become impassable.

If you find an inaccuracy in either the text or maps, please write to Crimson Publishing at the address below.

First published 2004 by Jarrold Publishing.

This edition first published in Great Britain 2009 by Crimson Publishing and reprinted with amendments 2017.

Crimson Publishing, 19-21C Charles Street, Bath, BA1 1HX

www.pathfinderwalks.co.uk

Printed in India by Replika Press Pvt. Ltd. 3/17

Front cover: River Dart estuary, Kingswear
Previous page: Hope Cove

Contents

Keymap

SCALE 1:500 000 or 1 INCH to about 8 MILES *1CM to 5KM*

0 2 4 6 8 10 12 14 16 KILOMETRES

0 2 4 6 8 10 MILES

KEYMAP HEIGHTS SHOWN IN METERS

Introduction

South Devon is justifiably a highly popular walking and holiday destination. It combines a mild climate and rugged coastline with superb beaches, rolling and unspoilt countryside, beautiful river valleys, delightful old towns and picturesque villages. What more could walkers wish for, especially as along the way there are thatched pubs dispensing pasties and cider and old tea shops tempting you with clotted cream teas, just rewards for a vigorous walk.

And let's face it, some of these walks – although short – are quite vigorous. South Devon's terrain is hilly and it is difficult to find a reasonably flat walk of any length. In the following selection of 20 walks, only four – Walks 1, 2, 5 and 18 – could be classified as flat. But the rolling hills, deep valleys, steep cliffs and dramatic coastline are the very reasons why walking in South Devon is such a pleasurable experience in any season of the year.

Fairlynch Museum, Budleigh Salterton

Boats on Sidmouth beach

For the purposes of this guide, South Devon is defined as the area roughly between the southern fringes of Dartmoor – and farther east the M5 motorway – and the sea. It can be divided into three main areas, defined by the numerous rivers which flow roughly north-south across it from the upland wilderness of Dartmoor. Moving from west to east, the first area is the South Hams, extending approximately between Plymouth and the River Dart. Next comes the area between the Dart and the Exe. This is Devon's main holiday area with a string of popular resorts that include Torquay, Paignton, Brixham, Teignmouth and Dawlish. East of the Exe and stretching to the Dorset border is East Devon. Here are more resorts – Exmouth, Budleigh Salterton, Sidmouth, Seaton and Beer – and another superb coastline.

South Hams

The South Hams is southernmost Devon, an almost triangular wedge of land which thrusts southwards into the English Channel. It is characterised by rolling well-wooded hills and deep river valleys which broaden out into long and winding estuaries. These estuaries – Plym, Erme, Avon, Salcombe and Dart – are its chief physical feature. Stretching westwards from the Dart Estuary is a rugged and majestic coastline, with steep cliffs overlooking sandy beaches, which offers some of the finest coastal walking in Britain.

This is thinly populated country. Kingsbridge, at the head of the Salcombe Estuary, is the chief town and is a relatively small – if bustling

– place. Nearby are delightful villages, many of which have fine churches. Despite the magnetic attraction of the coast, the hills and many river valleys of the South Hams should not be ignored. There is much pleasant walking here, providing variety and a contrast with the coastal routes.

Between Dart and Exe

This area contains Devon's main holiday coast around Tor Bay. The borough of Torbay – simply an administrative convenience – comprises the three main towns of Torquay, Paignton and Brixham, all of which are popular but in different ways. Torquay retains some fine Regency architecture and originally developed in the early 19th century as an aristocratic resort. Paignton, with its excellent sands, was always more of a family resort and the narrow streets and picturesque harbour of the old fishing port of Brixham, nestling below Berry Head, has always attracted thousands of visitors.

The Mew Stone near Berry Head

Because Torbay is built-up do not think that this is a chiefly urban coastline. Apart from the main seafronts, developments are mainly discreet and unobtrusive and there are well-wooded and totally unspoilt stretches of the South West Coast Path with little walking on tarmac, as revealed by Walk 15.

East of Torbay, the Coast Path continues to Shaldon and the broad Teign Estuary, then through the resort of Teignmouth and along more sandstone cliffs to Dawlish at the mouth of the Exe.

Bowling Green marshes, Topsham

East Devon

The coast between the Exe Estuary and the Dorset border has been declared a World Heritage Site because of its magnificent expanse of sandstone cliffs. Here the resorts – Exmouth, Budleigh Salterton, Sidmouth, Seaton, Beer – are smaller, quieter and generally more genteel. East of Beer the sandstone changes to chalk, a striking contrast which heralds the start of the Dorset coast.

Away from the excellent and often energetic walking along the coast, there are delightful inland routes in the Otter and Sid valleys and East Devon even has its own mini-Dartmoor, the gorse, tree and heather clad expanses of Woodbury Common. This surprisingly wild area is criss-crossed by paths and tracks and, because of its elevated position, gives fine views over the coast.

Exeter

Exeter has always been the main town and chief focal point of South
Devon. Originally founded by the Romans – some of whose walls still
survive – it developed into the administrative, military and religious
capital of the area. In the late 11th century the Normans began the
building of both the cathedral and castle and in the Middle Ages and
later, the city became an important wool-exporting port. The first ship
canal in England was constructed in Elizabethan times to prolong its
maritime life.

Nowadays the old refurbished quayside is one of many historic
attractions and, despite extensive wartime damage, Exeter is a rewarding
and fascinating city to explore.

Teign Estuary

Ayrmer Cove

Walking in the area

The main attraction for walkers in South Devon is obviously the magnificent coast, traversed throughout by the well-waymarked and well-maintained South West Way, and many of the finest stretches of this coast are featured in the selection of routes. *One word of caution is to take care when venturing onto the cliff tops and exposed headlands in strong winds, especially winter gales. What can seem a benign ramble on a calm summer day can be a rather more hazardous proposition on a blustery day in January and on such days, it is better to switch to a more sheltered inland walk.*

Inland, the paths are generally less frequently used and this means that, as well as getting muddy after wet weather, they may become overgrown during the summer. Neither of these are major problems.

At any time of the year, once away from the main resorts and popular beaches, whether striding along the Coast Path or on inland routes, you will find exhilaration, solitude and a true feel of remoteness.

1 *Stover Lake*

This short, easy and relaxing walk takes you through the attractive woodlands and around the shores of the lake at Stover Country Park. The park was part of the former estate of the Templer family and comprises around 114 acres of woodland, lake, marsh and heathland.

START Stover Country Park

DISTANCE 1½ miles (2.4km)

TIME 1 hour

PARKING Stover Country Park

ROUTE FEATURES Flat and easy walking through woodland and around a lake

Stover Lake

Begin in front of the Nature Interpretation Centre and take the path to the left of it, signposted To Templer Way, through woodland to a T-junction. Turn left, turn right at a sign to The Pinetum and turn right again at a T-junction. The path bends right between water both sides and at a T-junction in front of the lake, turn left onto the Newton Abbot to Bovey Tracey Cycle Route. Cross a bridge over a stream, turn left along a path and the path bends right and continues in a straight line, keeping more or less parallel with electricity pylons.

PUBLIC TRANSPORT Buses from Newton Abbot and Bovey Tracey

REFRESHMENTS None

PUBLIC TOILETS At start

ORDNANCE SURVEY MAPS Explorer OL44 (Torquay & Dawlish), Landranger 191 (Okehampton & North Dartmoor)

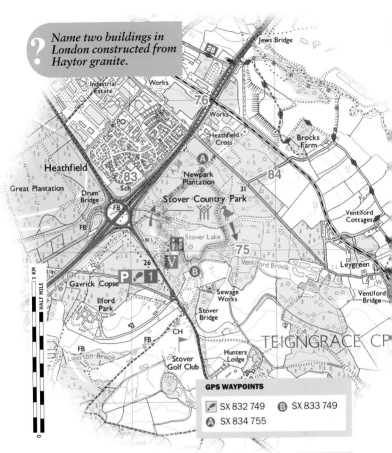

? Name two buildings in London constructed from Haytor granite.

GPS WAYPOINTS

🖌 SX 832 749   **Ⓑ** SX 833 749
Ⓐ SX 834 755

At a crossways **Ⓐ**, turn right along a path which brings you to Stover Lake. The remainder of the walk is a circuit of this most attractive stretch of water. Keep ahead over a bridge, continue beside the lake, following its curve to the right, and bear right across a boardwalk to a T-junction **Ⓑ**.

Stover Country Park is situated between Newton Abbot and Bovey Tracey. Its main feature, the 10-acre lake, has been designated as a **Site of Special Scientific Interest** and is particularly important for dragonflies and wildfowl. A new Nature Interpretation Centre, opened in 2000, has displays illustrating the wealth of animal and plant life in the park.

Looking across to Stover Lake

Turn right along a tree-lined path and turn left at another T-junction. At the next T-junction, turn left again to return to the start.

By the lakeside

The history of **Stover** is basically the story of the rise of the Templer family. It began with James Templer, a poor orphan in Exeter, who ran away to sea as a young man and made a fortune in India. On his return to England, he bought a large, rundown estate on the southern edge of Dartmoor in 1765 and began the building of **Stover House**, now a school, and the landscaping of the grounds. In 1792 his son – also called James – built the **Stover Canal** to carry clay from workings on the estate to the River Teign for export from Teignmouth. Later in 1820 his grandson, George Templer, constructed a tramway to bring granite from his quarries on Dartmoor to link up with the canal. By about 1850 the granite quarries had become uneconomic but clay continued to be transported along the canal until the 1950s.

Topsham and the Exe Estuary

START Topsham, Quayside
DISTANCE 2 miles (3.2km)
TIME 1 hour
PARKING Topsham
ROUTE FEATURES Flat and easy walking along roads and tarmac paths

2

Although a predominantly urban walk, close to the town and entirely on roads and tarmac paths, it does have a rural feel and there are fine and wide views across the marshes and mudflats of the Exe estuary to the Haldon Hills on the other side. Topsham is a fascinating and most attractive little town, well worth a thorough exploration.

Start at the Quay (by The Lighter Inn). Facing the river, turn left along the Strand. Where the road turns 90 degrees left, keep ahead along a tarmac path – this is the Goat Walk – on an embankment raised above the marshes and mudflats of the Exe estuary. The path bends left to emerge onto a lane Ⓐ (Bowling Green Road).

Keep ahead and just after the lane bends left, a gate on the right leads to a RSPB Nature Reserve viewing platform, from which there are fine

Attractive Topsham

PUBLIC TRANSPORT Buses and trains from Exeter and Exmouth
REFRESHMENTS Pubs and cafés at Topsham
PUBLIC TOILETS Topsham
ORDNANCE SURVEY MAPS Explorers 114 (Exeter & the Exe Valley) or OL44 (Torquay & Dawlish), Landranger 192 (Exeter & Sidmouth)

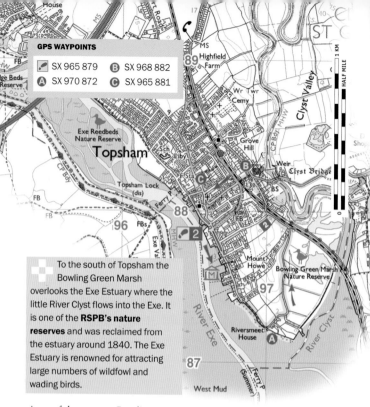

GPS WAYPOINTS

🖊 SX 965 879   Ⓑ SX 968 882
Ⓐ SX 970 872   Ⓒ SX 965 881

To the south of Topsham the Bowling Green Marsh overlooks the Exe Estuary where the little River Clyst flows into the Exe. It is one of the **RSPB's nature reserves** and was reclaimed from the estuary around 1840. The Exe Estuary is renowned for attracting large numbers of wildfowl and wading birds.

views of the estuary, Bowling Green Marsh and the confluence of the Exe and the Clyst. Continue along the lane, passing the RSPB hide. National Cycle Route 2 comes in from the right and joins the lane for a short stretch – *watch out for cyclists* as the lane ascends alongside the railway embankment. Stay on the lane as it bears right – now called Elm Grove Road – to cross a railway bridge. Keep ahead to join a main road Ⓑ and bear left.

Almost immediately turn left along an enclosed path. Go through a kissing-gate, cross the railway line, turn left to go through a gate onto a road and turn right. At a footpath sign to Town Centre, turn left along an enclosed tarmac track which becomes a road. Where it bends right, keep ahead to emerge into Fore Street opposite Topsham church and turn right.

Take the first street on the left

C (Exe Street), signposted to River and Ferry. At a T-junction, turn left along a narrow street beside the estuary, passing below the church, and follow it back to the start. ●

As you walk along the Goat Walk, which seaside resort can be seen ahead at the mouth of the estuary?

Topsham – just downstream from Exeter – was an important port in the Middle Ages and later, mainly involved in the exporting of wool. It remains a delightfully unspoilt small town with a wealth of old buildings and is particularly noted for its large number of 17th and 18th century houses, many built in the Dutch style. Some of these can be seen on the first part of the walk along the Strand and one of the finest of them now houses the **Topsham Museum**.

The Exe Estuary at Topsham

3 The Dart Valley Trail

START The Plains, Totnes
DISTANCE 3¼ miles (5.2km)
TIME 1½ hours
PARKING Car parks in Totnes
ROUTE FEATURES Surfaced driveway, field and woodland paths, some muddy after wet weather

Historic Totnes is one of south Devon's loveliest small towns, a popular centre for visitors and locals alike with a multitude of individual shops and tempting places to eat. Allow time to look around after this gentle walk, which escapes the bustle and follows the Dart Valley Trail south through peaceful countryside above the tranquil River Dart. The outward route is shared with cyclists, but is never busy.

Start from The Plains (once an area of tidal marsh: note the original granite posts for the town marsh gates) at the bottom of Totnes High Street by the monument in honour of William John Wills. With your back to the roundabout walk through The Plains, passing tastefully converted quayside warehouses; where the road bears right keep ahead, signed to the Steam Packet Inn. Follow footpath signs left to walk along the river's edge, with the Island opposite, bearing right to regain the road

The River Dart seen from the Dart Valley Trail

PUBLIC TRANSPORT Totnes is served by buses from a wide area, and is on the Exeter–Plymouth railway
REFRESHMENTS Pubs and cafés in Totnes; Steam Packet Inn passed on route
PUBLIC TOILETS Several in Totnes
ORDNANCE SURVEY MAPS Explorer OL20 (South Devon), Landranger 202 (Torbay & South Dartmoor)

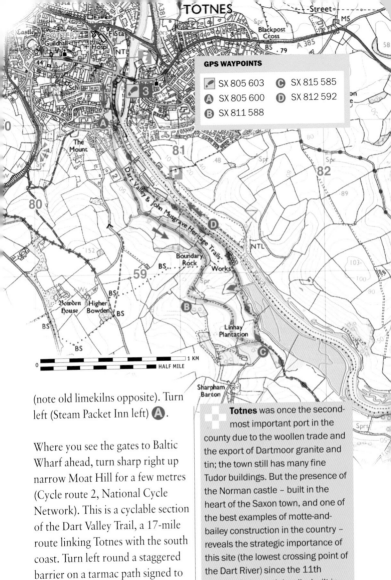

GPS WAYPOINTS

🚶 SX 805 603	**C** SX 815 585
A SX 805 600	**D** SX 812 592
B SX 811 588	

(note old limekilns opposite). Turn left (Steam Packet Inn left) **A**.

Where you see the gates to Baltic Wharf ahead, turn sharp right up narrow Moat Hill for a few metres (Cycle route 2, National Cycle Network). This is a cyclable section of the Dart Valley Trail, a 17-mile route linking Totnes with the south coast. Turn left round a staggered barrier on a tarmac path signed to Ashprington, soon joining the old driveway to Sharpham House and turning left.

Totnes was once the second-most important port in the county due to the woollen trade and the export of Dartmoor granite and tin; the town still has many fine Tudor buildings. But the presence of the Norman castle – built in the heart of the Saxon town, and one of the best examples of motte-and-bailey construction in the country – reveals the strategic importance of this site (the lowest crossing point of the Dart River) since the 11th century. Substantial walls, built in the 12th century, enclose the oldest part of the town.

Jersey cows on the Sharpham Estate in the Dart Valley

The driveway ascends gently and steadily, soon giving lovely views down the Dart. It runs along the top edge of beech woodland, the verges thick with ransoms in May. The way levels and passes through a kissing-gate next to a larger gate, then narrows and drops downhill through rolling parkland.

Pass through another gate **B** (note the 'Sharpham' plaque) and a strip of woodland. The next gate leads back into parkland, with beautiful

> **?** *How many miles is it from Totnes to Stokenham?*

views over the river and reedbeds and to the Sharpham estate beyond; you may also spot a Dart River river cruiser making its way gently downstream towards Dartmouth. The driveway bears left and descends gently.

Just by a gateway in the wall right – plus a public footpath sign **C** (Dart Valley Trail keeps straight on) – turn sharp left as signed across open pasture, dropping steeply towards the river to meet the bottom edge of the field. Turn left, soon bearing right as signed along the bottom edge, climbing to pass through a gate into a plantation of lime, sweet chestnut and cherry.

Today the **Sharpham Estate** is known for its excellent wines, made from grapes grown on the warm, sheltered slopes of the Dart Valley, and for its range of cheeses, formerly produced in the 18th-century coachyard (tours, café and shop). But the estate's earlier history is rather less mellow: although the farm dates back 1,000 years, Sharpham House as seen today was built between 1770 and 1824 for Captain Philemon Pownall of HMS *Favourite*, with prize money from the capture of a Spanish treasure ship. Sadly the whole estate was later gambled away by his grandson.

Leave the plantation over a stile and keep along the lower edge of the next field, then cross a stile into woodland and immediately descend a flight of wooden steps. The path crosses a boardwalk then continues along a damp stretch with snaking willows and yellow flags left, reed beds right. Climb to cross another stile and along the bottom of a meadow.

The next gate **D** leads back into woodland. At the end of the wood the path climbs steeply past a kissing-gate, then along the lower edge of field (fenced), with lovely views ahead of the tall pinnacled tower of St Mary's Church and the Norman castle keep to its left. Cross a stile and drop to meet a broad tarmac area (Baltic Wharf); turn left. Pass round the gates to regain the road by the Steam Packet Inn (St Peter's Quay), and retrace your steps to The Plains.

Looking downstream from Totnes Bridge; the river was first crossed at this point in the late 13th century

4 *Start Point*

START Start Point
DISTANCE 2 miles (3.2km)
TIME 1 hour
PARKING Start Point
ROUTE FEATURES Easy walking on the Coast Path around a headland

From the prominent headland of Start Point, there are magnificent and extensive views northwards across the wide sweep of Start Bay and westwards across Lannacombe Bay. The route follows a tarmac path along the north side of the point to the lighthouse at the tip and then continues along the dramatic south side before heading gently uphill across the neck of the headland to the start.

Begin by climbing the stone stile beside a gate at the far end of the car park and walk along an enclosed, gently descending tarmac path to the lighthouse at the tip of Start Point. Retrace your steps to a Coast Path sign **Ⓐ**.

Turn left onto a path which heads over the narrow headland and curves right to contour along the south side of Start Point. The path later descends to the base of the cliffs and curves right.

? What is the name of the organisation responsible for Britain's lighthouses?

An information board at the start of the walk points out the sites of the **lost villages of Start Bay**. These are former fishing villages that have been abandoned after being destroyed by the sea. They include Hallsands – just below the point – Slapton Cellars and Strete-Undercliffe.

At a fingerpost **Ⓑ** above the lovely cove of Great Mattiscombe Sand – where the Coast Path bends left – keep ahead to a gate. Go through, head gently uphill along an enclosed path, going through two more gates, and after the second one, turn left over a stone stile to the start. ●

PUBLIC TRANSPORT None
REFRESHMENTS None
PUBLIC TOILETS None
ORDNANCE SURVEY MAPS Explorer OL20 (South Devon), Landranger 202 (Torbay & South Dartmoor)

View towards Hallsands and Beesands from Start Point

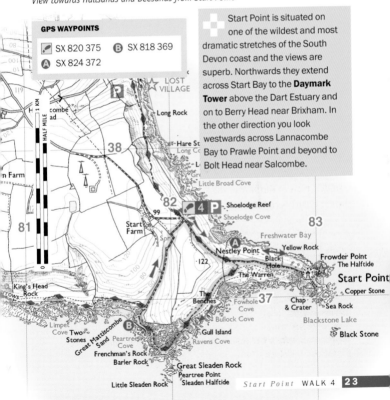

GPS WAYPOINTS

SX 820 375   **B** SX 818 369

A SX 824 372

Start Point is situated on one of the wildest and most dramatic stretches of the South Devon coast and the views are superb. Northwards they extend across Start Bay to the **Daymark Tower** above the Dart Estuary and on to Berry Head near Brixham. In the other direction you look westwards across Lannacombe Bay to Prawle Point and beyond to Bolt Head near Salcombe.

5 *Slapton: Nature Reserve and Village*

START Slapton Sands, Memorial car park
DISTANCE 3 miles (4.8km)
TIME 1½ hours
PARKING Slapton Memorial car park
ROUTE FEATURES Easy walking along paths through a nature reserve and by a lake

Although the walk starts on the coast by Slapton Sands, most of it is through a well-wooded nature reserve beside the lake of Slapton Ley. At about the halfway point, you pass through the quiet, attractive and interesting village of Slapton.

🥾 Turn right out of the car park, passing the memorial, and turn left along the lane signposted to Slapton. After crossing Slapton Bridge, turn left round a five-bar gate (viewing platform left) to enter the nature reserve. Follow an undulating path through trees either above or beside Slapton Ley – there is a series of gates and steps – eventually bending right away from the lake and continuing through woodland to a fingerpost and stile Ⓐ.

Climb the stile, keep ahead and the path bends left in front of a gate to

The memorial at Slapton Sands

PUBLIC TRANSPORT Buses from Dartmouth, Kingsbridge and Plymouth (to Torcross only, circa 1 mile south)
REFRESHMENTS Pubs at Slapton
PUBLIC TOILETS At start
ORDNANCE SURVEY MAPS Explorer OL20 (South Devon), Landranger 202 (Torbay & South Dartmoor)

In the tranquil surroundings of Slapton it is difficult to imagine that in the spring of 1944, the village – along with others in the locality – resounded with the noise of tanks and shelling as it was used as a training ground for **American troops** in preparation for the D-Day landings in Normandy. The villagers had to evacuate their homes for about seven months. Some of the buildings were destroyed and it took a long time for conditions to return to normal after the war. There is a fine medieval church and the ruined tower at the side of the Tower Inn is the only surviving remnant of a **College of Priests**, founded in 1373.

emerge from the trees and heads gently uphill. Climb a stile onto a tarmac track, go left uphill and through a gate onto a lane. Turn left **B**, head downhill through the village of Slapton.

As the lane bears sharp right at Sands Road Corner **C** (*go right here to find the two pubs, church and ruined tower*), bear left downhill. Soon after the lane starts

GPS WAYPOINTS

SX 828 442	**C** SX 821 449
A SX 821 443	**D** SX 820 448
B SX 824 448	

The memorial on Slapton Sands at the start of the walk is a tribute to which group of people?

to ascend, turn left **D** along a tarmac track, at a public footpath sign to Slapton Ley. Continue along a rough enclosed track – later by a right field edge – and descend gently to a gate. Go through and continue downhill along an enclosed path into the nature reserve again to a T-junction. Turn left along a path signed 'Permissive Path to Nature Reserve' and the route continues across a boardwalk and up steps to a T-junction. Turn right, **A** here rejoining the outward route, and retrace your steps beside Slapton Ley to the start.

Slapton Ley was originally a bay of the sea but is now cut off from it by a long ridge of shingle. It is the largest natural freshwater lake in the West Country and forms the centrepiece of a **National Nature Reserve,** surrounded by reed bed, marsh, shingle and attractive woodland.

Slapton Ley from Slapton Bridge

Woodbury Common

6

The route takes you across part of Woodbury Common, a large and surprisingly wild area of woodland and heath that lies to the north of Exmouth and Budleigh Salterton. It includes the highest point on the common, the tree-covered, prehistoric fort of Woodbury Castle, around 600 ft high and a superb vantage point over common and coast.

START Woodbury Common, Four Firs Cross, junction of B3180 and B3179
DISTANCE 3 miles (4.8km)
TIME 1½ hours
PARKING Four Firs Cross car park
ROUTE FEATURES Undulating walking across open heathland and through woodland

From the car park entrance, cross the lane and take the middle path opposite – there is a mauve waymark here. The path soon widens into a track and heads gently uphill across the gorse, bracken and heather of the common, keeping roughly parallel with the road on the left, to reach Woodbury Castle car park **A**.

? *Approximately between which dates was Woodbury Castle fort occupied?*

Woodbury Common

PUBLIC TRANSPORT None
REFRESHMENTS Ice-cream van at Woodbury Castle car park in season
PUBLIC TOILETS None
ORDNANCE SURVEY MAPS Explorer 115 (Exmouth & Sidmouth), Landranger 192 (Exeter & Sidmouth)

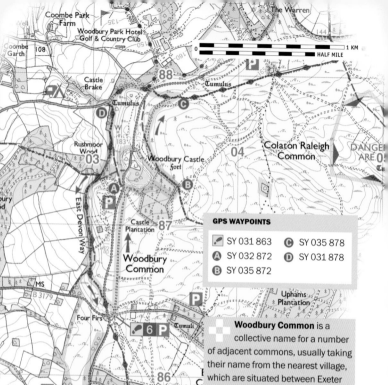

GPS WAYPOINTS

🖉 SY 031 863	Ⓒ SY 035 878
Ⓐ SY 032 872	Ⓓ SY 031 878
Ⓑ SY 035 872	

Woodbury Common is a collective name for a number of adjacent commons, usually taking their name from the nearest village, which are situated between Exeter and Honiton and just to the north of the coast. It is an area of rough, open heath and woodland, mostly owned by the Devon Clinton Estates, criss-crossed by tracks and footpaths and a paradise for walkers who wish for some of the 'wilderness experience' normally only achieved in South Devon by visiting Dartmoor. Numerous car parks make excellent starting points.

In the top right-hand corner of the car park, take the path to the right of an information board. The path curves right and soon reaches a T-junction. Turn left into trees and curve right through woodland (earthworks to left) eventually to cross a bank onto a track at the woodland edge. Turn left along this broad track by the right edge of woodland; at a crossways (blue sign) Ⓑ turn left and continue

along the right edge of trees. Follow the winding path to a T-junction. Turn right, continue across the open common (a sometimes wet area is crossed on boardwalks). At a fork take the left-hand path **C**.

About 200 yds farther on – and about 50 yds before the next waymarked fork – turn sharp left onto a clear path to the B3180. Cross over and take the lane opposite, passing the entrance to Woodbury Park Hotel, Golf and Country Club.

After a quarter of a mile, turn left **D**, at public bridleway and East Devon Way signs, along a woodland track. Following the (purple) East Devon Way signs all the time, continue along the track

Despite its name, **Woodbury Castle** is not a castle but a prehistoric hill fort. Although its extensive earthworks are covered by trees and severed by a road, they can still be traced. The fort stands at the highest point on the common, around 600 ft above sea level, and is a magnificent viewpoint.

and across more open common (view to the Exe Estuary right), ignoring paths to left and right. The track eventually curves left and heads gently uphill to the B3180 again. Cross over and take the path opposite which curves right to a track. Turn right and the car park is just ahead.

Wild woodland and heath at Woodbury Common

7 Aveton Gifford and the River Avon

START Aveton Gifford
DISTANCE 2¾ miles (4.4km)
TIME 1½ hours
PARKING Aveton Gifford, Timbers car park by bridge
ROUTE FEATURES Easy walking along lanes and paths by an estuary, through woodland, across fields and through a village

The first part of the route is along a lane by the estuary of the River Avon. You then walk through woodland above a creek and continue across fields to the village of Aveton Gifford. The final stretch is along the attractive village street. Please note that the first part of the walk beside the estuary is along a lane that is sometimes under water for a few hours either side of high tide. Please check with Kingsbridge Tourist Information Centre (Tel: 01548 853195) before setting out.

Turn right out of the car park along a lane and walk beside the Avon Estuary for a little over half a mile. *Take care as this is a narrow lane and it can be busy at times.*

On reaching a ford over a creek 🅐, bear right along a path below a wooded cliff which curves right beside the creek. Look out for where a yellow waymark directs you to bear right to climb a stile

The Avon Estuary

PUBLIC TRANSPORT Buses from Dartmouth, Kingsbridge and Plymouth
REFRESHMENTS Pub at Aveton Gifford
PUBLIC TOILETS None
ORDNANCE SURVEY MAPS Explorer OL20 (South Devon), Landranger 202 (Torbay & South Dartmoor)

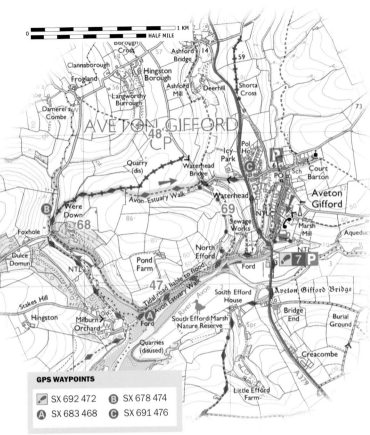

GPS WAYPOINTS

📍 SX 692 472   **B** SX 678 474
A SX 683 468   **C** SX 691 476

🏁 **Aveton Gifford** comprises little more than one long street (Fore Street) which stretches for about ½ mile from the church to the bridge over the River Avon. The cruciform church has a chunky, fortress-like appearance and its most unusual feature is the circular tower with a conical roof at the south west corner of the central tower. It was built in the 14th century and restored in the 1950s.

and continue through woodland, heading up to a T-junction. Turn left along a path to a lane and turn right **B**.

At a public byway sign to Drunkards Hill, bear right along an uphill, tree-lined track. The track levels out and on emerging into a small open area, turn right over a stile, bear left and walk diagonally

> **Why did the church at Aveton Gifford have to be restored after the Second World War?**

across the corner of a field to a stone stile. Climb it, turn right along the right field edge, follow the edge round to the left and at a hedge corner, continue downhill across the field, keeping along the left edge of a group of trees to a stile. Climb it, descend steps to a tarmac track, turn left and in front of a row of cottages, turn sharp right down a narrow lane. The lane bends left and continues uphill to the A379 **C**.

Cross carefully, turn left onto a tarmac path which bends sharply to the right and then turns left to a road. Keep ahead downhill under a canopy of trees to a T-junction and turn right. *At the next T-junction turn left uphill to visit Aveton Gifford church*; otherwise follow the road to the right through the village to the A379 again and cross over by a traffic island to return to the start. ●

The Devonian River Avon – less well-known than its namesakes in other parts of England – rises on Dartmoor and flows southwards across the South Hams into Bigbury Bay. South of Aveton Gifford it becomes tidal. A waymarked route – the Avon Estuary Walk – has been created along both sides of the estuary between Aveton Gifford, Bigbury-on-Sea and Bantham. The **ferry across the river at Bantham** enables it to be converted into a circular walk.

Aveton Gifford church

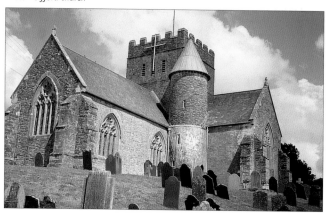

Berry Pomeroy

START Berry Pomeroy
DISTANCE 3 miles (4.8km)
TIME 1½ hours
PARKING Roadside parking at Berry Pomeroy
ROUTE FEATURES Easy walking along lanes, field paths and woodland tracks

Field paths, quiet lanes and tracks take you from the small village of Berry Pomeroy to the impressive remains of a castle, in an isolated location amidst woodland. There are fine views over the village and the Dart Valley on the return leg.

The walk starts at the crossroads in Berry Pomeroy. Turn down the road signposted to the church and where it bends right, turn left, at a public footpath sign, along an enclosed track. Pass between gateposts into a field and head gently uphill across it, veering slightly right away from the left edge and making for a gate in the far left-hand corner. Go through onto a road, turn right but almost immediately bear left along a lane signposted to Berry Pomeroy Castle and Afton.

? *Who began the building of Berry Pomeroy Castle?*

Berry Pomeroy church

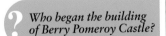

PUBLIC TRANSPORT Buses from Torquay, Totnes and Dartmouth
REFRESHMENTS Tearoom at Berry Pomeroy Castle
PUBLIC TOILETS None
ORDNANCE SURVEY MAPS Explorer OL44 (Torquay & Dawlish), Landranger 202 (Torbay & South Dartmoor)

Berry Pomeroy Castle has been owned by two families throughout its history, the Pomeroys and later the Seymours. The ruins, which occupy a cliff above a secluded wooded valley about 1 mile from the village and church, comprise two quite distinct parts: a medieval gatehouse and walls and an Elizabethan palace. Originally built in the 12th century, the Seymours decided to modernise it in the late 16th century and began the construction of an elaborate mansion. This was never completed and the castle was abandoned in the late 17th century and subsequently fell into ruin.

After a quarter of a mile, turn left at the castle entrance Ⓐ, climb a stile and walk gently downhill along a tarmac drive to the castle. Just before reaching the car park, bear left onto a path which heads downhill through woodland to a tarmac track. Turn right to a T-junction and turn right along a lane Ⓑ.

The lane heads uphill through woodland, levels off and descends to the castle entrance Ⓐ. Here you pick up the outward route and retrace your steps to the start. ●

Berry Pomeroy Castle

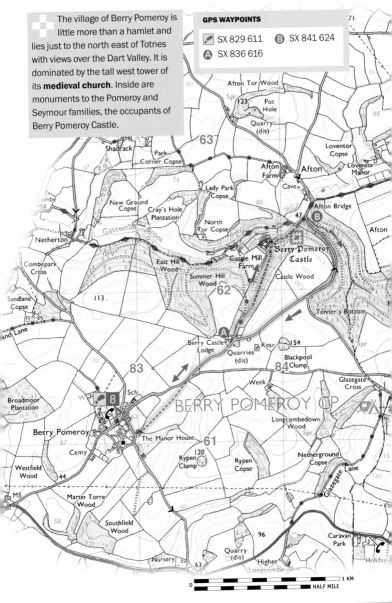

The village of Berry Pomeroy is little more than a hamlet and lies just to the north east of Totnes with views over the Dart Valley. It is dominated by the tall west tower of its **medieval church**. Inside are monuments to the Pomeroy and Seymour families, the occupants of Berry Pomeroy Castle.

GPS WAYPOINTS

SX 829 611   B SX 841 624

A SX 836 616

9 *Berry Head and Brixham*

START Berry Head Country Park

DISTANCE 3¾ miles (5.2km)

TIME 2 hours

PARKING Berry Head Country Park

ROUTE FEATURES Roads, tracks and coast path, one gentle climb

After an opening stretch along the coast above St Mary's Bay, the route heads inland across the neck of the headland and descends into Brixham. A walk beside the harbour is followed by an easy climb back onto Berry Head, passing the Napoleonic forts. There are grand views from the headland across Tor Bay and Start Bay.

Brixham harbour

Start by taking the lane to the right of the visitor centre and at a public footpath sign to Coast Path, turn left along an enclosed path to a stile. Climb it, keep by a wall on the left and climb a series of stone stiles as you follow the coast around Durl Head and above St Mary's Bay. Shortly after going through a kissing-gate you reach a fork **Ⓐ**.

> **?** *How high are the ramparts of the Northern Fort on Berry Head?*

PUBLIC TRANSPORT None to the start but Brixham is served by buses from Torquay, Paignton and Kingswear

REFRESHMENTS Pubs and cafés at Brixham, café at Berry Head North Fort

PUBLIC TOILETS At start, Brixham, Shoalstone Point, North Fort café

ORDNANCE SURVEY MAPS Explorer OL20 (South Devon), Landranger 202 (Torbay & South Dartmoor)

Take the right-hand enclosed tarmac path to a lane and keep ahead along Centry Road. Turn right at a crossroads, follow the road around a left bend and head down Ranscombe Road to a T-junction in the centre of Brixham **B**.

The two substantial stone forts on Berry Head were built during the **Napoleonic Wars** to protect Torbay, an anchorage for the British fleet, from an expected French invasion. At their height they were home to up to 1000 troops and 50 horses. The Northern Fort is the best preserved and the former guardhouse there is now a café.

GPS WAYPOINTS

✏	SX 940 561	**C**	SX 936 567
A	SX 933 555	**D**	SX 947 565
B	SX 928 563		

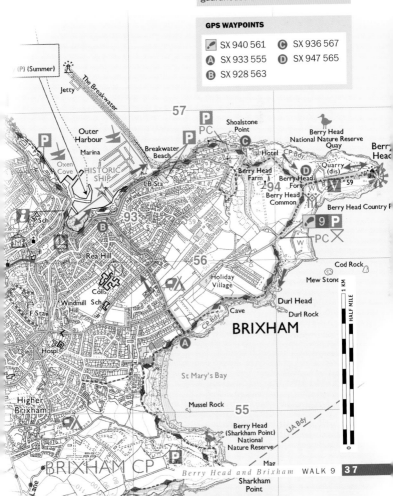

The main town and harbour are to the left but at the T-junction the route continues to the right along Berry Head Road beside the harbour. After about half a mile, turn left along a tarmac path and on reaching Shoalstone car park, turn right through it.

Turn left along Berry Head Road and follow it around a right bend and at a Berry Head Country Park sign, turn left through a kissing-gate. Continue through woodland, climb steps and head steadily uphill to emerge onto the open cliff top. Keep ahead – later along a tarmac track – to a T-junction **D**.

Turn left to enter the Northern Fort and keep ahead to the lighthouse on the tip of the headland. Retrace your steps to the T-junction and keep ahead, in the Southern Fort and Visitor Centre direction, and the track leads back to the start, passing to the right of the Southern Fort.

For generations a boat trip across the bay to **Brixham** has become an essential part of a holiday at the nearby resorts of Torquay and Paignton. It is still a working port and retains the atmosphere of a traditional fishing village, with narrow streets and rows of colourful houses and cottages rising steeply from the harbour. In 1688 Brixham played a major role in British history when **William of Orange** landed here at the start of his successful campaign to win the throne from his father-in-law, **James II**. There is a statue to him by the harbour.

Fort on Berry Head

Dittisham and the River Dart

START Dittisham, The Ham car park
DISTANCE 3¾ miles (5.2km)
TIME 2 hours
PARKING The Ham car park
ROUTE FEATURES Lanes, tracks and field paths, several short climbs

The starting point is a beautiful spot adjoining meadows beside the River Dart. From there you head up into the attractive village of Dittisham, walk beside a creek and continue along quiet, narrow lanes. On the final part of the route, which is a steady climb across fields, there are superb views over the winding Dart and the valley to the southern edge of Dartmoor.

🖊 Head uphill along the tarmac track to a road and bear left into Dittisham, passing the fine medieval church. At a T-junction in the village centre, turn right, not along the road but down steps. Continue downhill along a lane between thatched cottages. The lane bends left, heads uphill and curves right to the road. Head downhill along the road and keep beside a creek at the bottom.

At a public footpath sign, turn right over a plank footbridge Ⓐ. Cross

Dart Valley near Dittisham

PUBLIC TRANSPORT Occasional buses from Dartmouth and Totnes, ferry (Easter to October) from Dartmouth
REFRESHMENTS Pubs at Dittisham
PUBLIC TOILETS At start
ORDNANCE SURVEY MAPS Explorer OL20 (South Devon), Landranger 202 (Torbay & South Dartmoor)

Dittisham church

The steep, narrow streets of Dittisham lie amid rolling hills on the west bank of the River Dart. Dominating the village is the imposing church, which dates mainly from the early 14th century although the tall west tower is probably older. An unusual feature for a village church is the two-storied south porch.

At a sign to Kingston **B**, follow the narrow lane around a left bend. Head uphill, bending left, and then continue downhill to another left bend at the bottom.

another footbridge into woodland, cross a track, ascend steps, climb a stile and turn left along the bottom edge of a sloping field. Climb a stile and keep ahead along an attractive, tree-lined path. Climb another stile onto a lane and turn left downhill. After crossing a bridge the lane bends left uphill and you turn right along a lane signposted to Coombe.

Just after the left bend, turn right over a half-hidden stile **C** to the right of a gate. Turn left and walk initially along the right field edge, by a hedge on the right. Bear right, head uphill across the field, skirting the end of a hedge on the left, and continue more steeply up to a waymarked post. Bear left, continue – still uphill – by the right edge of the field and over the brow a magnificent view unfolds over the Dart Valley, with the uplands of Dartmoor on the horizon. After climbing a stile, head gently down by the right field edge to a kissing-gate, go through and continue down a tree-lined track to a road. Turn right into Dittisham and retrace your steps to the car park.

The winding **Dart** is considered to be one of the most beautiful rivers in England. Formed by the junction of the East Dart and West Dart – both of which rise on Dartmoor – it flows southwards from the moor through the historic town of Totnes. Between Totnes and Dartmouth comes the loveliest part of the valley: the river meanders between steep hillsides and wooded slopes and there are attractive villages close to its banks.

? *Which king of England has his coat of arms above the door inside Dittisham church?*

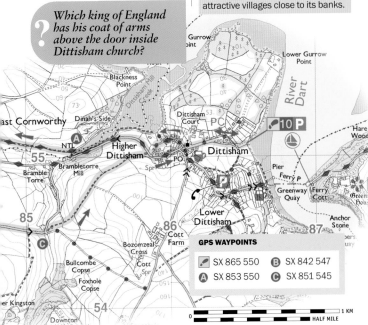

GPS WAYPOINTS

🖊 SX 865 550	**B** SX 842 547	
A SX 853 550	**C** SX 851 545	

0   1 KM
         HALF MILE

11 Torcross and Beesands

There are superb views over Start Bay and Slapton Ley both at the start and end of the route. In between, there is attractive walking through woodland, you pass through the small, isolated coastal village of Beesands and a relaxing stroll beside the beach precedes the final climb over the wooded headland of Dun Point. This is a fairly energetic walk with two climbs: the first is long – 1 mile – but gradual, the second is shorter but steeper.

START Torcross

DISTANCE 3½ miles (5.6km)

TIME 2 hours

PARKING Torcross

ROUTE FEATURES An undulating and well-wooded route – *quite steep in places* – with a flat stretch beside the sea

Beesands

Turn right out of the car park along the road into the village and where the road bends right, keep ahead along an uphill lane beside the Torcross Tavern. The lane bends right and continues steadily uphill, passing Torcross Viewpoint, from where there is a superb vista over Slapton Ley and Start Bay.

? *On what date was the Sherman tank at the side of the car park recovered from the sea?*

PUBLIC TRANSPORT Buses from Dartmouth, Kingsbridge and Plymouth

REFRESHMENTS Pubs and cafés at Torcross, pub at Beesands

PUBLIC TOILETS Torcross and Beesands

ORDNANCE SURVEY MAPS Explorer OL20 (South Devon), Landranger 202 (Torbay & South Dartmoor)

After ¾ mile – where a narrow lane comes in from the right – turn left through a kissing-gate **(A)**, at a public footpath sign to Beeson. Head uphill across a field – later by woodland on the right – go through a kissing-gate in the corner and turn left along a tarmac track. At a fingerpost, turn right (signposted Beeson) along a well-waymarked path through woodland to a stile. Climb it, continue downhill along the left edge of fields and go through a gate in the bottom corner of the last field. Cross a track and, keeping to the left of a farmhouse, walk along an enclosed track to reach two gates. Go through the right-hand gate and

Torcross is situated beside the sea at the southern end of the freshwater lake of Slapton Ley. After being recovered from the sea many years after the war, the Sherman tank in the car park was placed here as a memorial to more than 900 American servicemen, killed by a surprise **German attack** in April 1944 while rehearsing for the D-Day landings. News of the tragedy was suppressed at the time and it remained largely unknown until a local man, **Ken Small**, wrote a book about it and played a major role in organising the tank memorial.

continue along an undulating tree-lined path which widens into a track and emerges onto a lane. Turn left through the hamlet of Beeson.

Tank memorial at Torcross

GPS WAYPOINTS

SX 823 422   **B** SX 812 407
A SX 810 420   **C** SX 819 405

At a T-junction **B**, turn
left again along a lane. From here
there are grand views of the coast
and Widdicombe Ley. Head
downhill, follow the lane around
first a left bend and then a right
bend and at a T-junction, turn left
into Beesands.

The lane bends right through the
village but the route continues to
the left along a straight track **C**
alongside the beach. For the rest of
the walk you follow the regular
Coast Path signs. At a waymarked
post, follow the track to the left,

passing to the left of a house, and continue uphill along a narrow, enclosed path. The climb through woodland over the headland is quite a steep one and there are steps in places. After going through a gate, head gently downhill along the left edge of a field to another gate, go through that one and continue down an enclosed path. The path – which becomes a tarmac one – bends sharply to the right, then sharply left and at a

The remote fishing village of **Beesands** is little more than a line of cottages and a pub beside a flat stretch of coast. It has always been vulnerable to flooding and its latest sea defences were completed in 1993. Just to the north is the lake of **Widdicombe Ley**, a smaller version of Slapton Ley.

footpath post, turn right along a track. Turn left down steps and at the bottom, keep ahead to return to the start.

Slapton Ley from Torcross

12 *Wembury Bay*

START Wembury Marine Centre, Wembury Beach	
DISTANCE 4 miles (6.4km)	
TIME 2½ hours	
PARKING National Trust car park Wembury Beach	
ROUTE FEATURES Woodland and field paths, easy coast path with stunning views	

Standing on the Coast Path near Warren Point on a hot summer's day, gazing down at the deep turquoise-blue waters dotted with smart white sailing craft, you could be forgiven for thinking you had been whisked away to some Mediterranean idyll. But not so – this walk, starting from Wembury Beach and later following the South West Coast Path, explores a very special part of the South Devon coast.

Note that alternative parking is available on the road near the Post Office ●.

From the Marine Centre descend towards the beach, passing the café and toilets. Just above the sands turn right along the Coast Path to reach a footpath post via a footbridge. Turn right through a gate ❶ (Devon Coast to Coast path/Erme–Plym Trail) and head upvalley. Cross a footbridge and ascend to a gate onto a road; turn left to a T-junction. Cross over to find a bridleway that ascends a concrete drive, then levels and runs through woodland. The wooden bungalows peeping through the trees across the valley are holiday accommodation. Reach a lane and turn left, downhill.

At the bottom, turn right on a footpath ❷, passing a house. Head up a narrow path to a junction. Take the right path, soon crossing a stile and emerging into a

---

PUBLIC TRANSPORT Buses from Plymouth and Yealmpton
REFRESHMENTS Old Mill Café, The Odd Wheel PH
PUBLIC TOILETS Wembury Beach
ORDNANCE SURVEY MAPS Explorer OL20 (South Devon), Landranger 201 (Plymouth & Launceston)

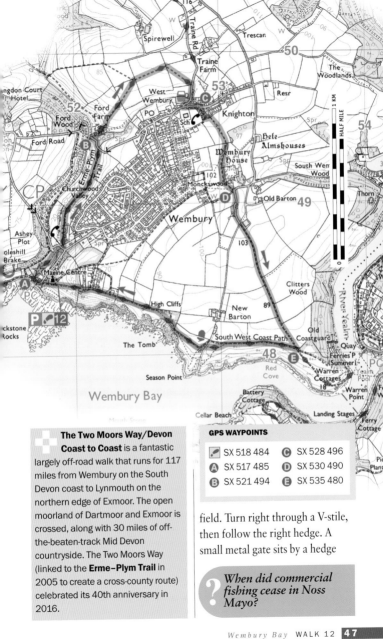

The map shows the area around Wembury Bay, including Spirewell, Traine Rd, Trescan, Traine Farm, The Woodlands, West Wembury, Knighton, Ford Wood, Ford Farm, Hele Almshouses, Wembury House, South Wem Wood, Churchwood Valley, Monckswood, Old Barton, Wembury, Ashey Plot, Coleshill Brake, Marine Centre, High Cliffs, New Barton, Clitters Wood, Old Coastguard, South West Coast Path, The Tomb, Season Point, Red Cove, Warren Cottages, Cellar Beach, Battery Cottage, Landing Stages, Warren Point, River Yealm, and Wembury Bay.

The Two Moors Way/Devon Coast to Coast is a fantastic largely off-road walk that runs for 117 miles from Wembury on the South Devon coast to Lynmouth on the northern edge of Exmoor. The open moorland of Dartmoor and Exmoor is crossed, along with 30 miles of off-the-beaten-track Mid Devon countryside. The Two Moors Way (linked to the **Erme–Plym Trail** in 2005 to create a cross-county route) celebrated its 40th anniversary in 2016.

field. Turn right through a V-stile, then follow the right hedge. A small metal gate sits by a hedge

? **When did commercial fishing cease in Noss Mayo?**

Pay a visit to the **Church of St Werburgh**: the view across the bay is wonderful. Dedicated to the daughter of Wulfhere, the first Christian King of Mercia, the building stands on the site of a Saxon oratory. The prominent early 15th-century tower acted as a navigation mark for sailors for many years. Wembury sits on the 630-mile **South West Coast Path**, which runs from Minehead in Somerset to Poole Harbour in Dorset.

gap; bear half left across the next field to a path junction. Keep ahead through the middle of the next field and the next hedge gap. Bear right diagonally across the next sloping field, keeping right of the telegraph pole, and descend to a kissing-gate onto a lane. The Devon Coast-to-Coast Path goes left; turn right, downhill, soon ascending to a T-junction by The Odd Wheel pub. Turn left on Knighton Road.

Just before the Post Office **C** turn right on a fenced footpath. At the path T-junction turn left, soon ascending steps into a field. Head across, and through the allotments. Pass through an iron kissing-gate by a substantial stone wall (enclosing the grounds of historic Wembury House), and then another, into open grassland. Stay alongside the wall as it curves left, eventually negotiating a kissing-gate and stone stile to reach a path junction and lane on a bend **D**.

Bear right along the lane. Where it bears away right, keep ahead through a gate on a track ('link to Coast Path'). Eventually start to descend, with views left to Newton Ferrers, and right to the mouth of the Yealm and the Great Mew Stone. Pass through a gate by a cottage (formerly housing lifesaving equipment) to reach the Coast Path (yellow arrows/acorn symbol) above Warren Point.

Turn right through a gate **E** and follow the Coast Path towards Wembury. Odd gates along the way enclose areas for conservation grazing by Dartmoor ponies. Below New Barton Farm, at a fork, take the left path (green arrow), which runs nearer to the sea and soon rejoins the main path, with lovely views west towards Wembury Point and Rame Head (south east Cornwall).

Continue along the path, through occasional gates, ignoring footpaths leading right. Pass below St Werburgh's church (accessed via a path, right, through a kissing-gate), then descend steps into the car park.

Budleigh Salterton and West Down

START Budleigh Salterton
DISTANCE 4 miles (6.4km)
TIME 2 hours
PARKING Budleigh Salterton
ROUTE FEATURES Easy, steady climbing along the Coast Path and field paths

From the centre of Budleigh Salterton, a steady climb over wooded cliffs brings you to the fine viewpoint of West Down Beacon, 423 ft high. A semi-circular walk across the down – much of it now occupied by a golf course – leads back to the Coast Path for the descent to the start.

The walk starts in front of the Fairlynch Museum. Facing it, turn right to the sea front and at a Coast Path sign, turn sharp right onto a tarmac path beside the stony beach. The path rises steadily and after going up steps, turn left in front of a door. Turn right, left again at a T-junction and then right again and where the tarmac path ends, keep ahead along the left edge of an open, grassy recreation area. Continue steadily uphill along an enclosed path over the cliffs, through gorse, bracken and trees, to West Down Beacon, the highest point.

Budleigh Salterton

At a waymarked post – just after the path starts to descend and by a triangulation pillar **A** on the right – turn right along a path which winds across more gorse, bracken and trees on West Down. On

PUBLIC TRANSPORT Buses from Exmouth and Sidmouth
REFRESHMENTS Pubs and cafés at Budleigh Salterton
PUBLIC TOILETS Budleigh Salterton
ORDNANCE SURVEY MAPS: Explorer 115 (Exmouth & Sidmouth), Landranger 192 (Exeter & Sidmouth)

Apart from a few old cottages, the resort of **Budleigh Salterton** is very much a creation of the 19th century. Handsome Victorian houses rise up from the long flat beach that extends from the mouth of the River Otter to the east to the cliffs on the west side and the town has a pleasantly old-fashioned air. It gets its name from the salterns or salt pans in which sea water used to be evaporated. **The Fairlynch Museum,** housed in an early 19th-century thatched house – one of a number built in the area – is well worth a visit.

emerging onto the corner of the East Devon golf course, bear slightly right away from its left edge to a footpath post and turn right between trees to a T-junction.

Turn left gently downhill along an enclosed track, later continuing along the left edge of the course, and where the track bears right, keep ahead along an enclosed path to a kissing-gate. Go through and walk across a field to a fingerpost on the far side **B**.

Turn right – the path is signposted Littleham Church Path – along the left field edge and go through a kissing-gate in the corner. Turn right across another small area of the golf course and then continue gently downhill along an enclosed path. Cross a track and keep ahead – later through woodland – to the B3178.

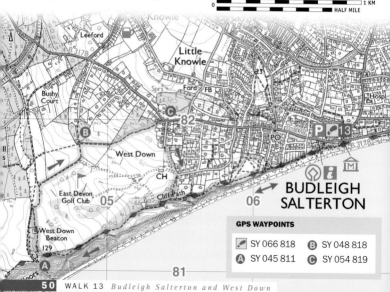

GPS WAYPOINTS

🖊 SY 066 818		**B** SY 048 818	
A SY 045 811		**C** SY 054 819	

Red cliffs to the west of Budleigh Salterton

Turn right and immediately turn right again along Links Road **C**, heading uphill. Follow the road around left and right bends, pass to the left of the golf club car park and at the next left bend, turn right, at a public footpath sign, onto a path which curves left along the left edge of the course again to a footpath post. Keep ahead gently downhill through trees and bracken to a T-junction and turn left onto the Coast Path. Here you rejoin the outward route and retrace your steps to the start.

The superb views from **West Down Beacon** extend over much of East Devon and along the South Devon coast to the cliffs at Berry Head beyond Brixham. The granite tors of Dartmoor can be seen on the horizon and nearer at hand is the resort of Exmouth and the open heathlands of **Woodbury Common**.

Otter Estuary Nature Reserve

Otterton Ledge

Which estuary can be seen from the path across West Down, just after leaving the Coast Path?

14 *Bigbury-on-Sea, Ringmore and Ayrmer Cove*

START Bigbury-on-Sea
DISTANCE 4 miles (6.4km)
TIME 2 hours
PARKING Bigbury-on-Sea
ROUTE FEATURES Several ascents and descents – *some quite steep* – along tracks, field paths and the Coast Path

An undulating inland stretch across fields brings you to the picturesque village of Ringmore and from there an enclosed path leads to the coast at Ayrmer Cove. The last 1¼ miles is a superb roller-coaster walk along a dramatic section of the south Devon coast, with views ranging across Bigbury Bay to Bolt Tail and Wembury Head.

From the car park head up to the road and keep ahead uphill along Parker Road. Where the road ends, climb a stile and continue up over the brow of the hill along the right edge of three fields.

In the corner of the third field Ⓐ, turn left and head downhill along the right field edge to a gate. Go through and continue steeply downhill along the left edge of the next two fields to a track at the bottom. Bear left to a waymarked

Ayrmer Cove

PUBLIC TRANSPORT Occasional buses from Kingsbridge and Plymouth
REFRESHMENTS Pub at Ringmore, beach cafés (seasonal) at Bigbury and Challaborough
PUBLIC TOILETS At start
ORDNANCE SURVEY MAPS Explorer OL 20 (South Devon), Landranger 202 (Torbay & South Dartmoor)

post, follow a path uphill across a field, climb a stile and descend steps to a lane. Go through the gate opposite, head downhill along the right edge of a field and in the corner, cross a footbridge over a brook and climb a stile. Walk uphill through a young plantation, go through a gate, continue up along an enclosed path and go through a kissing-gate onto a track. Turn

right, immediately turn left, go through a hedge gap and keep along the left edge of a field. After going through a kissing-gate in the corner, walk along a hedge-lined path to a tarmac track and keep ahead into the village of Ringmore. At a T-junction, turn right along a lane through the village.

Turn left in front of the church **B** and at a fork in front of the pub, take the left hand uphill lane. Turn right along a tarmac track and look out for where a public bridleway sign directs you to bear left along a tree-lined path to a gate. Go through and continue along an enclosed path which bends first to the right and then to the left and heads steadily downhill to Ayrmer Cove.

Bigbury-on-Sea and Burgh Island

At a fingerpost 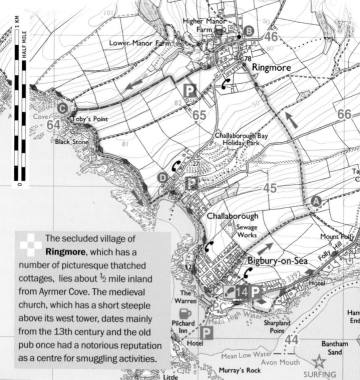, turn left onto the Coast Path and head steeply up over the cliffs. The path then descends to the beach at Challaborough, bending sharply left above the sands to emerge onto a track. Turn left to the road.

Turn right alongside the beach **D** and where the road bends left, keep ahead along an ascending path. Go through a gate, keep ahead to a road and walk down into Bigbury. At a Coast Path sign, bear slightly right down steps and the path leads back to the start. ●

> **?** Which famous writer of thrillers used to stay at the hotel on Burgh Island in the 1920s and 30s?

GPS WAYPOINTS

🖉 SX 651 442		**C** SX 641 455
A SX 657 448		**D** SX 648 450
B SX 652 459		

The secluded village of **Ringmore**, which has a number of picturesque thatched cottages, lies about ½ mile inland from Ayrmer Cove. The medieval church, which has a short steeple above its west tower, dates mainly from the 13th century and the old pub once had a notorious reputation as a centre for smuggling activities.

Walls Hill, Hope's Nose and Lincombe Woods

START Babbacombe, Walls Hill (cricket) car park
DISTANCE 5½ miles (8.8km)
TIME 3 hours
PARKING Walls Hill car park (fee-paying)
ROUTE FEATURES Mainly along cliff top and woodland paths with small stretches of road walking, some moderate climbs

Despite being wholly within the built-up area of Torbay, this is a most attractive and unspoilt walk that embraces both splendid cliff top walking and some delightful woodland. It is an undulating route so expect several modest ascents and descents. From the Coast Path there are superb and extensive views over Tor Bay to Berry Head and across Babbacombe Bay towards Teignmouth.

Begin by taking the path that leads off from the far end of the car park, pass beside a barrier and continue over the cricket pitch to a Walls Hill noticeboard. Continue over the downs, with views to Teignmouth on the left, and on reaching the clifftop keep ahead to meet a Coast Path post **A**.

Bear right along the clifftop, soon curving right along the edge of Anstey's Cove. At a Coast Path sign continue along an enclosed path through woodland, turn left down steps, then turn right and head downhill – more steps in places – to a lane. Turn left and level with Anstey's Cove car park, turn left beside a barrier, at a Coast Path sign **B**, onto a path through more delightful woodland.

The next stretch is called the Bishop's Walk. Follow the undulating Coast Path, pass beside a barrier and keep ahead along a tarmac drive which bends right to

PUBLIC TRANSPORT Buses from Teignmouth and Torquay
REFRESHMENTS Pubs and cafés at Babbacombe, café at Kent's Cavern
PUBLIC TOILETS None en route
ORDNANCE SURVEY MAPS Explorer OL44 (Torquay & Dawlish), Landranger 202 (Torbay & South Dartmoor)

a road. Cross over and at a 'Coast Path, Hope's Nose' sign, turn left onto an uphill grassy path parallel to the road. The path becomes enclosed, curves right, continues up through trees and finally descends to a road **C**.

For the detour to Hope's Nose, cross over, climb a stile and take the downhill path ahead. Go through a gate and continue on down to the end of the promontory.

Retrace your steps to the road, turn left and follow the coast road around a right bend. On reaching an open grassy area dotted with bushes, tall conifers and benches, turn left along its left edge and go through a hedge gap to Thatcher Point. Ahead is the prominent landmark of Thatcher Rock. Follow the Coast Path to rejoin the road **D**.

GPS WAYPOINTS

✎	SX 928 652	**D**	SX 940 632
A	SX 935 650	**E**	SX 935 633
B	SX 935 645	**F**	SX 934 639
C	SX 944 635		

? *Who manages Anstey's Cove?*

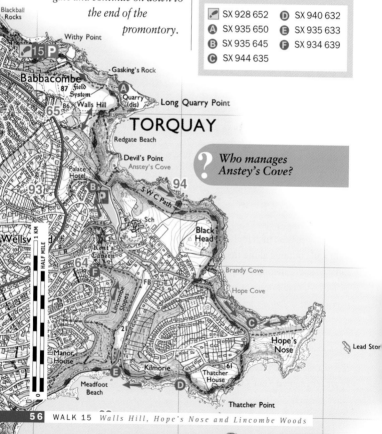

Above Anstey's Cove

At the gates to Woodhey **F** (right), turn right at a fingerpost down a narrow path in the Kent's Cavern direction, head first downhill, then climb steps and keep ahead to pass Kent's Cavern. Continue through the car park, then down steps to a road.

Turn left downhill, eventually passing traffic lights at a single-track section. About 100 yds before reaching a T-junction (pink cottage right) turn left down steps, keep ahead to cross a car park and go up steps on to a road **E**.

Cross the road, pass through a wall gap and barrier opposite and take the path ahead. At the first path junction turn left and pass through a hedge gap, then turn immediately right and continue along the inside right edge of Lincombe Woods. *Note: In summer parts of this path may be overgrown, in which case it is possible to walk along the left edge of the grassy area to the right, soon crossing a footbridge to join the woodland path.* Later the path bears left, signed Kent's Cavern, and heads uphill through the trees.

Cross over and turn right downhill. Where the road bears right, turn left – there is a public footpath sign to Anstey's Cove – along a tarmac path. Continue along the left edge of an open grassy area and on through Anstey's Cove car park to a lane **B**. Turn left to rejoin the outward route and retrace your steps to the start. ●

> **Kents Cavern** has been attracting visitors for more than a century. The caves were first excavated in the 1860s and guided tours tell you about the prehistoric animals that used to roam here, the caves and how the Victorian explorers and archaeologists uncovered their treasures and secrets. There is a visitor centre, shop and café.

16 *Shaldon and the Teign Estuary*

START Shaldon

DISTANCE 4½ miles (7.2km)

TIME 2½ hours

PARKING Shaldon, The Ness car park

ROUTE FEATURES Flat and easy walking beside the estuary is followed by several fairly steep climbs and descents along lanes, tracks and the Coast Path

The first part of the walk is mainly along tarmac paths beside the Teign Estuary between Shaldon and Ringmore. You then turn inland for an 'up and down' stretch along narrow lanes, green roads and paths, passing the superb 554 ft high viewpoint of The Beacon. The final leg heads downhill along the Coast Path and over the wooded headland of The Ness, with dramatic views across the estuary to Teignmouth and beyond.

Turn left out of the car park and follow the lane through the attractive village. Where the lane bears left, keep ahead, passing to the right of a war memorial clock tower, and turn right at a crossroads. The lane curves left beside the Teign Estuary to the main road by Teignmouth and Shaldon Bridge **A**.

Cross over and keep ahead along a tarmac track beside the estuary which curves left away from the river to a road. Turn right into Ringmore and the road bends left uphill through the village, passing to the left of the small 17th-century church. At a right bend, keep ahead along a lane (Higher Ringmore Road) which heads uphill between thatched cottages.

About 200 yds beyond the last of the houses, turn right **B** onto a hedge-lined track. The track winds uphill to a T-junction. Turn right down a tarmac track to a lane, turn

PUBLIC TRANSPORT Buses from Exeter, Teignmouth and Torquay, ferry from Teignmouth

REFRESHMENTS Pubs and cafés at Shaldon

PUBLIC TOILETS Shaldon

ORDNANCE SURVEY MAPS Explorer OL44 (Torquay & Dawlish), Landranger 192 (Exeter & Sidmouth)

left uphill and on the brow of the hill, turn left again onto another hedge-lined track. This is a green road called Butterfly Lane and you follow it steadily uphill to emerge onto a lane at the viewpoint of The Beacon and a triangulation pillar **C**.

Turn left downhill and at a public footpath sign at the bottom, turn right over a stile. Head gently downhill along a fence-lined path which bears right to a stile. Climb it and keep ahead, over another stile and through a gate, to emerge onto the A379. Turn right and although you have to walk along it for only about 200 yds, *take great care as it is a busy main road, there are no verges and it is quite narrow.*

GPS WAYPOINTS

✎ SX 938 719	**C** SX 931 709
A SX 931 724	**D** SX934 709
B SX 926 716	

In the 19th century the **River Teign** was a busy commercial waterway. Granite from Dartmoor and clay were transported down the river to the port of Teignmouth, across the estuary from Shaldon, and from there shipped to London or exported. Like its smaller neighbour Shaldon, Teignmouth is now mainly a holiday resort.

At the first bend **D**, turn sharp left along a track to a stile – here joining the Coast Path – climb the stile and head downhill along the right edge of a field. Pass through a hedge gap and as you continue steeply down, there is a magnificent view ahead over Shaldon, the Teign Estuary and Teignmouth. In the bottom corner of the field, go up steps to climb a stile, walk along an enclosed path, go through a hedge gap and continue along the right edge of a golf course. At the next corner, keep ahead through woodland and descend steps to a track. Turn right downhill and at a fork, take the right hand path through Ness Woodland. At the next fork, continue along the right hand path heading over the headland of The Ness to another superb viewpoint. Turn left, descend through the trees, by a wire fence on the right, go down steps and turn left alongside the shore to a lane. Turn left to return to the car park. ●

> **?** *In which year was the first wooden bridge built across the Teign Estuary between Teignmouth and Shaldon?*

The Ness and Teignmouth

Bolt Tail and Bolberry Down

17

START Outer Hope, Hope Cove car park
DISTANCE 5 miles (8km)
TIME 2½ hours
PARKING Hope Cove car park
ROUTE FEATURES A fairly easy stretch of the Coast Path followed by lanes and tracks

Hope Cove is a particularly attractive settlement and there are beautiful and dramatic coastal views on the first part of the walk, especially across Bigbury Bay, as you follow the Coast Path through Hope Cove and around the headland of Bolt Tail before heading over the cliffs of Bolberry Down. The route then turns inland and follows mainly quiet, narrow lanes and tracks back to the start.

🖉 Turn left out of the car park through the picturesque hamlet of Outer Hope, passing to the right of the Beachcomber café and to the left of the post office, and where the road ends keep ahead along a tarmac path. Climb steps, keep ahead to emerge onto a lane and head downhill along it to a road in Inner Hope. Bear right and where the road bends left, keep ahead up a flight of steps. The path continues to a kissing-gate. Go through, head steadily uphill through woodland to emerge onto open downland and continue up

The ramparts of the Iron Age fort on **Bolt Tail** are still clearly visible and probably date from around 600BC. They were built across the neck of the peninsula to guard the fort from the landward side. Similar forts are to be found on many of Britain's coastal headlands.

towards the headland of Bolt Tail to reach a Coast Path post **A**. Either bear left to the next post, or bear right through the ramparts of a prehistoric fort. Keep ahead, then bear left along the cliffs (*exposed*) to rejoin the Coast Path by another post, and keep ahead. Follow a

PUBLIC TRANSPORT Infrequent buses from Kingsbridge
REFRESHMENTS Pubs and cafés at Hope Cove, hotel bar at Bolberry Down, cream teas/lunches at Burton Farmhouse
PUBLIC TOILETS Hope Cove
ORDNANCE SURVEY MAPS Explorer OL20 (South Devon), Landranger 202 (Torbay & South Dartmoor)

grassy path uphill along the cliff edge and descend slightly to a gate. Pass through and continue uphill, with a fence on the left. Go through a gate  **B** at the top and continue across the open expanses of Bolberry Down. The path eventually bends left away from the cliffs and at a fork, take the left-hand path – here leaving the Coast Path – and continue along a tarmac path.

Pass beside a barrier, turn right to a car park **C** and turn left along a lane. Descend steeply to a T-junction, turn left and at a fork, take the right-hand narrow, winding lane downhill through the hamlet of Bolberry. The lane continues uphill.

Where it bends right **D**, keep ahead, at a footpath sign to Sweethearts Lane and Galmpton, along a narrow enclosed path. This may be overgrown at times. Reach a T-junction, turn left along a track towards a house; at a public footpath sign to Galmpton and Hope Cove, turn right up steps and walk along an enclosed path to a stile. Climb it, head uphill across a field, climb another stile and turn right along a field edge track.

Immediately after going through a gate, turn left over a stone stile **E** and walk along a track which keeps along the left edge of a succession

Bury Stone
Bolt Tail
Wolf Rock
China Rock
edrot Cove
t Ledge

Hope Cove

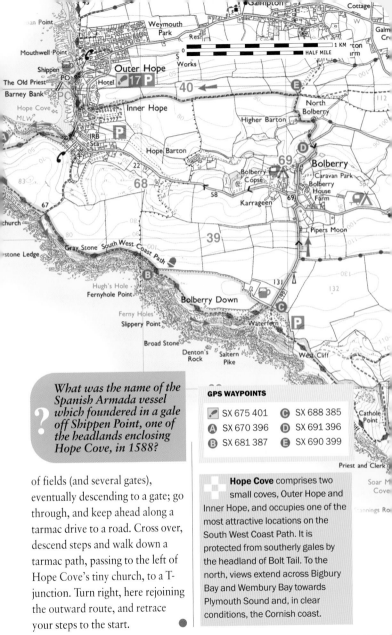

GPS WAYPOINTS

📍 SX 675 401   **C** SX 688 385

A SX 670 396   **D** SX 691 396

B SX 681 387   **E** SX 690 399

What was the name of the Spanish Armada vessel which foundered in a gale off Shippen Point, one of the headlands enclosing Hope Cove, in 1588?

of fields (and several gates), eventually descending to a gate; go through, and keep ahead along a tarmac drive to a road. Cross over, descend steps and walk down a tarmac path, passing to the left of Hope Cove's tiny church, to a T-junction. Turn right, here rejoining the outward route, and retrace your steps to the start.

Hope Cove comprises two small coves, Outer Hope and Inner Hope, and occupies one of the most attractive locations on the South West Coast Path. It is protected from southerly gales by the headland of Bolt Tail. To the north, views extend across Bigbury Bay and Wembury Bay towards Plymouth Sound and, in clear conditions, the Cornish coast.

18 Ottery St Mary and the River Otter

START Ottery St Mary
DISTANCE 6 miles (9.7km)
TIME 3 hours
PARKING Ottery St Mary
ROUTE FEATURES Easy walking along tracks and field paths, much of it through riverside meadows; ¾ mile along vergeless road

Apart from an opening stretch across fields, most of the walk is through woodland and across delightful meadows beside the River Otter. Note however that there is an unavoidable stretch of road on the outward route. Historic interest is provided by the magnificent medieval church at Ottery St Mary.

🥾 The walk starts from the church steps at the top of Silver Street. Walk down Silver Street, eventually curving left into The Square. Turn right; cross Hind Street, and turn right down the next street. At the junction bear left on Mill Street to pass Raleigh House (right); it is thought that a 16th-century house on this site may have been home to Sir Walter Raleigh.

Just before the road bears right to cross the river bear left **Ⓐ** down a track to find a footpath sign, and

through a gate. Almost immediately bear left along the top of an embankment. At a footpath post turn left down steps and keep straight on. The path eventually crosses a bridge; bear right uphill,

River Otter

PUBLIC TRANSPORT Buses from Sidmouth, Honiton and Exeter
REFRESHMENTS Pubs and cafés at Ottery St Mary
PUBLIC TOILETS Ottery St Mary (near church)
ORDNANCE SURVEY MAPS Explorer 115 (Exmouth & Sidmouth), Landranger 192 (Exeter & Sidmouth)

The medieval church at Ottery St Mary

then along the edge of a big field, then pass a gate into woodland. At the end of the wood descend steps, go through a gate and bear left along the field edge; pass through a five-bar gate to reach a path junction **B**.

Bear right and go through a small gate. Walk along an enclosed path, turning left to climb steps up an embankment and continue along the top of the embankment. After climbing a stile, turn right along the right edge of a field, go through a gate and continue along an enclosed track which emerges into a field. Walk along its right edge, turn right over two stiles in the corner and descend steps, then bear left to continue by the River

Otter. Cross a footbridge, keep ahead through trees beside the river and through a gate.

Turn left up a track **C** (unfortunately a short stretch of the path paralleling the river and shown on the OS map is no longer passable), which meets the road at Wiggaton. Turn right along the road *(take care – there is neither verge nor pavement)*.

At Lancercombe Farm **D** turn right as signed on a footpath to cross a bridge and pass through a gate; the path runs along the right edge of the field, bearing left as the river is approached. Cross a stile and pass through a kissing-gate, then along the right edge of a field

In the 18th century **Ottery St Mary** was an important wool centre and the town has a number of handsome Georgian buildings. The monument at the start of the walk, erected to commemorate Queen Victoria's Diamond Jubilee, is a copy of a gatepost at Kensington Palace. The poet **Samuel Taylor Coleridge**, was born here in 1772.

and over a stile. Pass through the edge of a removals depot, then keep to the left of old mill buildings to reach a footbridge over the river 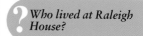.

Turn right to cross the river and turn right again. The return leg to Ottery St Mary is mainly along pleasant riverside meadows, keeping by the Otter most of the way and negotiating a series of footbridges and gates. The route is well-waymarked and there is just one place where you leave the river to cut off a bend, before the path picks up the trackbed of the old railway line to Sidmouth. Finally turn right over the Millennium Footbridge, and bear left on a path to regain the road at 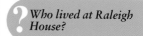. Turn right and follow the road into Ottery St Mary. Where the main road bends left, keep ahead along Mill Street into The Square and turn left to return to the start. ●

? Who lived at Raleigh House?

Meadows beside the Otter

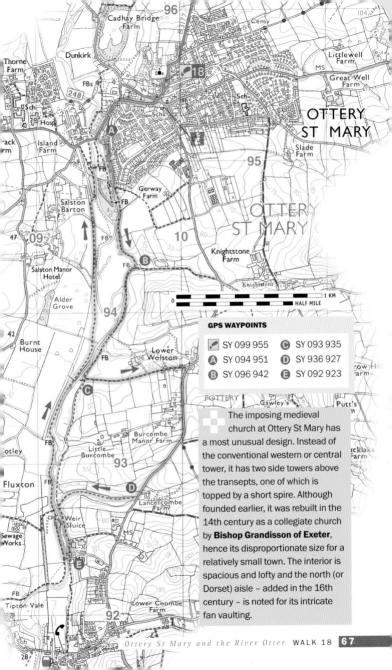

GPS WAYPOINTS

📍	SY 099 955	**C**	SY 093 935
A	SY 094 951	**D**	SY 936 927
B	SY 096 942	**E**	SY 092 923

The imposing medieval church at Ottery St Mary has a most unusual design. Instead of the conventional western or central tower, it has two side towers above the transepts, one of which is topped by a short spire. Although founded earlier, it was rebuilt in the 14th century as a collegiate church by **Bishop Grandisson of Exeter**, hence its disproportionate size for a relatively small town. The interior is spacious and lofty and the north (or Dorset) aisle – added in the 16th century – is noted for its intricate fan vaulting.

19 *Sidmouth and Ladram Bay*

START Sidmouth

DISTANCE 5½ miles (8.9km); shorter version 2½ miles (4km)

TIME 3 hours (1½ hours for shorter walk)

PARKING Sidmouth

ROUTE FEATURES Mostly along the Coast Path with two inland stretches, *lots of cliff walking with two fairly steep climbs*

The walk between Sidmouth and Ladram Bay provides continuously magnificent views, both inland over rolling countryside and in both directions along the coast. The highlight is the superb cliff scenery and interesting rock formations at Ladram Bay. The route is well-waymarked and easy to follow but fairly energetic.

The walk starts on the sea front at the corner of Fore Street and the Esplanade. Facing the sea, turn right and follow the road as it bears right uphill, later quite steeply. Where the road bears slightly right, keep ahead beside a gate, at a Coast Path sign, continue uphill along an enclosed tarmac path and pass beside another gate to rejoin the road.

At a public footpath sign opposite a car park on the right Ⓐ, turn left through a kissing-gate and walk along the left edge of two fields. Before reaching the corner of the second field, bear right across to a waymarked post Ⓑ on the far side.

Near Sidmouth

PUBLIC TRANSPORT Buses from Exeter, Exmouth and Honiton

REFRESHMENTS Pubs and cafés at Sidmouth, pub at Ladram Bay

PUBLIC TOILETS Sidmouth

ORDNANCE SURVEY MAPS Explorer 115 (Exmouth & Sidmouth), Landranger 192 (Exeter & Sidmouth)

Turn left if doing the short walk; for the full walk turn right – now on the Coast Path – to continue along the field edge. The path descends, via steps in places, to a kissing-gate. Go through, keep ahead along an enclosed path and go through another kissing-gate. Walk across a field, heading down into a dip and up again, go through a kissing-gate at a fingerpost and continue along the right inside edge of woodland.

At the next fingerpost **C**, keep ahead – here leaving the Coast Path – along a track which becomes hedge-lined and continues to a lane. Turn left and head gently downhill along an enclosed tarmac track – this is technically a public road. Follow it around a right bend to a T-junction and turn left to Ladram Bay.

At a three-way fork **D**, take the left hand tarmac path, here rejoining the Coast Path and keeping on it for the rest of the walk. The path curves left in front of the Three Rocks Inn and continues along the right edge of a play and picnic area to a kissing-gate. Go through, walk uphill

> As you walk westwards along the coast path from Sidmouth, the dramatic **red cliffs** at **Ladram Bay** soon come into view. Not only are the cliffs among the finest on the South Devon coast, but there are also a number of detached rock pillars, the home of thousands of sea birds.

Ladram Bay

along the right edge of a field, curving left and heading up to another kissing-gate in the corner. After going through that one, climb steps and continue over the wooded headland of High Peak to a T-junction **C**. Turn right – here temporarily rejoining the outward route – and retrace your steps as far as point **B** where you rejoin the shorter version of the walk. Keep ahead to a kissing-gate which admits you to the National Trust's Peak Hill property. Continue along a path which winds steeply downhill through woodland and along the cliff edge, finally descending steps to a road. Turn

right, here rejoining the outward route again, and retrace your steps down the road and along the promenade to the start.

Sidmouth, a resort noted for its gentility, occupies a sunny and sheltered position between steep sandstone cliffs at the mouth of the little River Sid. It became fashionable during, and just after, the Napoleonic Wars when the English aristocracy were cut off from their usual continental haunts and the town possesses a number of dignified Georgian and Regency villas. **Queen Victoria** stayed here as a young girl with her parents in 1819.

Cliffs near Sidmouth

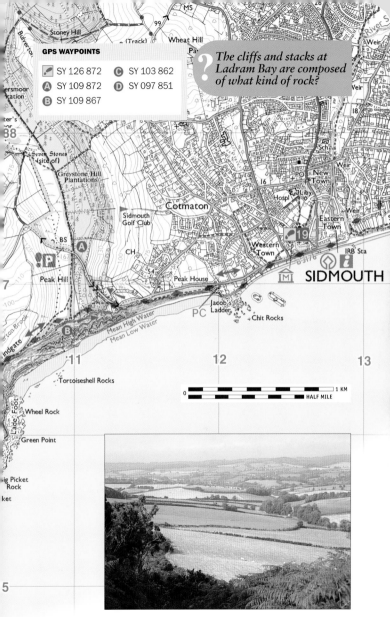

GPS WAYPOINTS

SY 126 872
A SY 109 872
B SY 109 867
C SY 103 862
D SY 097 851

The cliffs and stacks at Ladram Bay are composed of what kind of rock?

Rolling countryside near Sidmouth

20

Kingswear and the Dart Estuary

START Kingswear

DISTANCE 6 miles (9.6km)

TIME 3 hours

PARKING Darthaven Marina car park, Kingswear (fee)

ROUTE FEATURES Hilly tracks and an 'up and down' Coast Path, fairly strenuous

An opening ramble along the Coast Path above the well-wooded estuary of the River Dart is followed by an inland stretch, mainly along clear and well-surfaced tracks. The return follows a highly scenic but fairly strenuous section of the Coast Path. Both on the inland and coastal sections there is quite a lot of climbing but the views are outstanding, especially looking across the estuary to Dartmouth. Apart from the twin castles at Dartmouth and Kingswear, further historic interest is provided by the Daymark Tower and Brownstone Battery.

Dartmouth from Kingswear

Turn right out of the car park and walk along the road through Kingswear to the railway station. Where the road reaches the ferry slip, keep ahead under an arch and turn left up Alma Steps, at a Coast Path sign. At the top, turn right along a tarmac drive, eventually heading steadily uphill, and the drive narrows to a path which emerges onto another drive. Walk along this winding, tree-shaded drive to where the Coast Path turns right **A**.

PUBLIC TRANSPORT Buses from Brixham and Paignton, ferries from Dartmouth

REFRESHMENTS Pubs and cafés at Kingswear

PUBLIC TOILETS By ferry slip, Kingswear

ORDNANCE SURVEY MAPS Explorer OL20 (South Devon), Landranger 202 (Torbay & South Dartmoor)

Brownstone Battery

Keep ahead along the drive, in the Brownstone direction, and at a fork, take the right-hand lower track. At a public footpath sign just in front of a house, turn right down a track and then continue steeply uphill along a stony path by the edge of woodland. The path emerges via a gate onto a track; continue uphill, passing to the left of Higher Brownstone Farm.

Soon after turn right as signed **B**, in the Coast Path direction, along a hedge-lined track. The track heads uphill and on meeting a tarmac way, bear right along it. Follow it around a right bend, pass to the right of the prominent Daymark

Tower – a stile and path give access to it – and head downhill towards the sea. Go through a kissing-gate to enter the National Trust's Froward Point property and continue downhill to reach the Second World War defences of Brownstone Battery (note the visitor centre left). Give yourself some time to climb down to the look-out below the point, which once housed a searchlight.

At a Coast Path sign turn right **C** in the Kingswear direction, passing through woodland to reach a squeeze stile. Go through and then follow a steep and winding 'up and down' stretch to a stile. Climb it

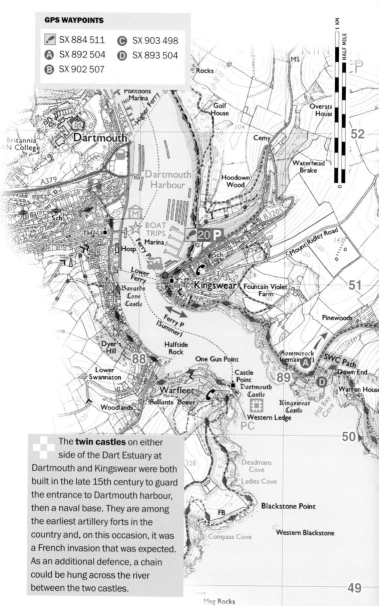

GPS WAYPOINTS

- ✏ SX 884 511
- Ⓐ SX 892 504
- Ⓑ SX 902 507
- Ⓒ SX 903 498
- Ⓓ SX 893 504

The **twin castles** on either side of the Dart Estuary at Dartmouth and Kingswear were both built in the late 15th century to guard the entrance to Dartmouth harbour, then a naval base. They are among the earliest artillery forts in the country and, on this occasion, it was a French invasion that was expected. As an additional defence, a chain could be hung across the river between the two castles.

and as you continue through delightful woodland, grand views open up on the left of the Dart estuary and both Dartmouth and Kingswear castles. The path later bends right uphill, then goes left and descends steeply, via steps in places, to a tarmac track. Turn right and at a Coast Path sign, turn left **D** along an enclosed path to a stile. Climb it, ascend a long flight of steps through woodland, cross a track and continue up more steps.

Brownstone Battery, now maintained by the National Trust, is one of the few surviving Second World War coastal defences. It was built in 1940 to protect the Dart Estuary and Slapton and Blackpool Sands from an anticipated German invasion and was manned by around 300 soldiers. Although lacking the picturesque qualities of a ruined castle, the remains are fascinating and they form an integral part of Britain's history.

At the top, turn left onto a tarmac drive **A**, here rejoining the outward route, and retrace your steps to the start.

? *What was the purpose of the Daymark Tower?*

Above the Dart Estuary

Further Information

Walking Safety

Always take with you both warm and waterproof clothing and sufficient food and drink. Wear suitable footwear, such as strong walking boots or shoes that give a good grip over stony ground, on slippery slopes and in muddy conditions. Try to obtain a local weather forecast and bear it in mind before you start. Do not be afraid to abandon your proposed route and return to your starting point in the event of a sudden and unexpected deterioration in the weather.

All the walks described in this book will be safe to do, given due care and respect, even during the winter. Indeed, a crisp, fine winter day often provides perfect walking conditions, with firm ground underfoot and a clarity of light unique to that time of the year.

The most difficult hazard likely to be encountered is mud, especially when walking along woodland and field paths, farm tracks and bridleways – the latter in particular can often get churned up by cyclists and horses. In summer, an additional difficulty may be narrow and overgrown paths, particularly along the edges of cultivated fields. Neither should constitute a major problem provided that the appropriate footwear is worn.

Follow the Country Code

- Be safe – plan ahead and follow any signs
- Leave gates and property as you find them
- Protect plants and animals, and take your litter home
- Keep dogs under close control
- Consider other people

(Natural England)

Useful Organisations

Campaign to Protect Rural England
Tel. 020 7981 2800
www.cpre.org.uk

National Trust
Devon Regional Office
Tel. 01392 881691
Membership and general enquiries
Tel. 0344 800 1895
www.nationaltrust.org.uk

Natural England
Tel. 0300 060 3900
www.gov.uk/government/organisat
ions/natural-england

Ordnance Survey
Tel. 03456 05 05 05
www.ordnancesurvey.co.uk

The Ramblers
Tel. 020 7339 8500
www.ramblers.org.uk

South West Coast Path Association
Tel. 01752 896237
www.southwestcoastpath.org.uk

Youth Hostel Association
Tel. 01629 592700
www.yha.org.uk

Local Organisations
Devon County Council
Tel. 0345 155 1015
www.devon.gov.uk

South Devon AONB Unit
Tel. 01803 861384
www.southdevonaonb.org.uk

Local Tourist Information Centres
Brixham, Paignton and Torquay:
01803 211211
www.englishriviera.co.uk
Budleigh Salterton: 01395 445275
www.visitbudleigh.com
Dartmouth: 01803 834224
www.discoverdartmouth.com
Dawlish: 01626 621665
www.visitsouthdevon.co.uk

Exeter: 01392 265700
www.exeter.gov.uk
Exmouth: 01395 830550
www.exmouth-guide.co.uk
Honiton: 01404 43716
www.visithoniton.com
Newton Abbot: 01626 215667
www.visitsouthdevon.co.uk
Ottery St Mary: 01404 813964
www.otterystmarytourism.org.uk
Plymouth, Mayflower Centre:
01752 306330
www.plymouth.gov.uk
Salcombe: 01548 843927
www.salcombeinformation.co.uk
Sidmouth: 01395 516441
www.visitsidmouth.co.uk
Teignmouth: 01626 215666
www.visitsouthdevon.co.uk
Totnes: 01803 863168
www.totnesinformation.co.uk

Public Transport
For all public transport enquiries:
Traveline. Tel. 0871 200 2233
www.traveline.org.uk
National Rail Enquiries
Tel. 08457 484950
www.nationalrail.co.uk

Ordnance Survey Maps
The walks described in this guide
are covered by Ordnance Survey
1:50 000 scale (1¼ inches to 1 mile
or 2cm to 1km) Landranger map
sheets 191, 192, 201, 202. These

all-purpose maps are packed with information to help you explore the area. Viewpoints, picnic sites, places of interest and caravan and camping sites are shown, as well as public rights of way information such as footpaths and bridleways.

To examine the area in more detail, and especially if you are planning walks, the Ordnance Survey Explorer maps at 1:25 000 scale (2½ inches to 1 mile or 4cm to 1km) are ideal. Maps covering the area are:

OL20 (South Devon)
OL44 (Torquay & Dawlish)
114 (Exeter & the Exe Valley)
115 (Exmouth & Sidmouth)
116 (Lyme Regis & Bridport)

Answers to Questions

Walk 1: Any two of these – London Bridge, British Museum, National Gallery.

Walk 2: Exmouth.

Walk 3: 17 miles (27km); on National Cycle Network Notice on staggered barrier soon after Ⓐ.

Walk 4: Trinity House.

Walk 5: To the local people of Slapton and other villages in the South Hams – for giving up their homes to aid the war effort in the Second World War.

Walk 6: Between 500 and 300BC (on information board in castle car park).

Walk 7: Because it was almost destroyed in an air raid in 1943.

Walk 8: Ralph de Pomeroy, a supporter of William the Conqueror.

Walk 9: 18 ft (5.5m)

Walk 10: Charles II.

Walk 11: May 19, 1984.

Walk 12: 1960s (from an information board near Warren Point, Ⓔ).

Walk 13: The estuary of the River Exe.

Walk 14: Agatha Christie.

Walk 15: Torbay Coast and Countryside Trust (notice in Anstey's Cove car park).

Walk 16: 1827.

Walk 17: *San Pedro el Major* (answer found on an information board above the beach at Outer Hope).

Walk 18: Dr Edward Davy (1806–85), pioneer of the electric telegraph (plaque on house).

Walk 19: Sandstone.

Walk 20: It was built as an aid to navigation along the South Devon coast and is still in use today.

Ordnance Survey

Pathfinder® Guides | **Britain's best-loved walking guides**

South West of England
Pathfinder Walks

Short Walks

South East of England
Pathfinder Walks

Short Walks

Practical Guides

GPS FOR WALKERS
MAP READING SKILLS
THE COUNTRYSIDE COMPANION

For more information visit

www.pathfinderwalks.co.uk
tel: 01225 584 950
email: info@pathfinderwalks.co.uk
Twitter: @PathfinderWalks
Facebook: www.facebook.com/pathfinderwalks